MASTERING FRUGALITY: EFFECTIVE STRATEGIES FOR SAVING MONEY

Unlock Financial Freedom and Build Wealth with Practical Money-Saving Techniques

I0427212

Dr. Kirsten Amanda

The information contained in this publication is safeguarded by copyright law and must not be replicated, duplicated, or transmitted in any manner without obtaining explicit consent from the author or publisher.

Under no circumstances will the author or any contributors be held responsible for compensation, damages, or financial loss, whether occurring directly or indirectly as a result of the content presented in this publication.

Legal Disclaimer:

This publication is intended solely for personal use. Any alteration, distribution, sale, utilization, reproduction, or transmission of any portion or material from this publication without obtaining permission from the author or publisher is strictly prohibited.

Disclaimer

The information provided in this book, is intended for general informational purposes only. The author and publisher make no representations or warranties of any kind, express or implied, about the completeness, accuracy, reliability, suitability, or availability of the information contained herein.

The techniques and strategies discussed in this book are based on the author's research and personal experiences. While efforts have been made to provide accurate and up-to-date information, financial circumstances can vary widely, and what works for one individual or situation may not work for another.

Readers are encouraged to consult with financial advisors, professionals, or experts before making any significant financial decisions or implementing any of the strategies discussed in this book. The author and publisher disclaim any liability for any financial or personal loss, damage, or inconvenience that may arise as a direct or indirect result of using the information presented in this book.

Furthermore, the author and publisher do not endorse or promote any specific products, services, or companies mentioned within the book. Any references or recommendations are for illustrative purposes only and should not be considered as endorsements.

Readers should use their discretion and judgment when applying the principles and advice provided in this book. It is essential to take into account one's unique financial situation, goals, and needs. The responsibility for any financial decisions or actions taken based on the content of this book lies solely with the reader.

This book once again, is intended as a guide to help readers explore various strategies for managing their finances more effectively. It is not a substitute for professional financial advice, and readers should exercise caution and seek personalized guidance when making important financial choices.

<u>Dedication</u>

All those who dare dream of financial freedom…

This book is dedicated to very individual with unwavering determination, resilience and determination to achieve a better future through smart financial choices is an inspiration to us all Let these pages be your guiding light on your journey to financial literacy. With every tip, every insight, and every strategy shared within, you will discover the tools and knowledge you need to shape your financial destiny.

In pursuing financial commitment, you may discover not only the joy of saving but also the power that comes from taking control of your financial well-being Your dedication to this path is a testament to your vision, and we salute your efforts.

With heartfelt thanks in your pursuit of financial wisdom, freedom and peace that come from wise financial choices.

TABLE OF CONTENT

Dr. Kristen Amanda

Introduction

Understanding Frugality

Have you ever thought of the word "frugal" as been miser to yourself, denying yourself the good life you want or being cheap? That is not the case if I may answer your bothering questions, the answer is no! You can still enjoy life to the fullest. But it is going to involve you being mindful of expenses and resource management.

Being frugal is all about efficient resource management, but it doesn't necessarily mean living a life of extreme deprivation or self-denial as I have explained earlier, it is based on "austerity". Austerity typically involves strict, self-imposed limits on spending, often to the detriment of one's quality of life, while frugality aims for balance and sustainability.

Frugality is a philosophy or way of life that emphasizes the careful and deliberate management of resources, especially finances, to achieve specific goals such as saving money, reducing debt, or achieving financial independence.

The Benefits of Being Frugal

There are a lot, I mean a lot of benefits of being frugal. Being frugal offers a multitude of advantages that extend beyond mere financial savings. Embracing a frugal lifestyle can significantly impact various aspects of your life, fostering personal growth, reducing stress, and contributing to a more sustainable and purposeful existence. Below are the key benefits of being frugal in which you certainly might not find in any book about frugality:

- **Financial Freedom:** This is perhaps the most apparent benefit, frugality enables you to gain control over your finances. By carefully managing expenses, saving money, and reducing debt, you can work toward financial independence and security. This freedom allows you to pursue your life goals and dreams with **"greater ease and peace of mind"**.

- **<u>Reduced Stress:</u>** Financial stress is a common source of anxiety for many individuals especially married couple. 60% to 85% of divorce in marriage is **money.** Frugality can alleviate this stress by providing a sense of stability and predictability in your financial life reducing divorce statistics. Knowing that you have savings and a plan for managing your money can lead to reduced stress and improved mental well-being, Interesting.

- **<u>Improved Financial Health:</u>** Being frugal often involves making wise financial decisions, such as prioritizing essential expenses, reducing unnecessary spending, and saving for the future, having an emergency fund: is a financial safety net or a savings account specifically set aside to cover unexpected or unforeseen expenses and emergencies which serves as a cushion to help individuals and households cope with financial setbacks without resorting to borrowing money, incurring debt, or depleting other essential savings. These practices contribute to better financial health, including a stronger credit score and a lower risk of financial crises.

- **<u>Sustainable Living</u>**: Frugality often aligns with principles of sustainability and environmental consciousness. By consuming less, repurposing items, and reducing waste; by fixing a partially damage item instead of replacing them, frugal individuals contribute to a more sustainable planet and a reduced carbon footprint.

- **<u>Enhanced Creativity:</u>** Living frugally encourages creativity and resourcefulness. Finding innovative ways to save money, repurpose items, or DIY(Do it Yourself) solutions not only saves money but also stimulates your problem-solving abilities and fosters a sense of accomplishment.

- **<u>Increased Appreciation:</u>** When you adopt a frugal lifestyle, you tend to develop a deeper appreciation for the things you have. You value your possessions, experiences, and relationships more, as you become more conscious of their value.

- **<u>Debt Reduction:</u>** Frugality often goes hand-in-hand with strategies for reducing and eliminating debt. By focusing on debt repayment especially paying up your highest debt first, you free up more of your income for savings and investments, ultimately improving your financial future.

- **<u>Time for What Matters:</u>** By avoiding excessive consumerism and time-consuming pursuits, you can prioritize activities that truly matter to you. This might include spending more quality time with loved ones, pursuing hobbies, or engaging in personal development activities.

- **Resilience:** Frugal individuals tend to be more resilient in the face of financial challenges.Warren Buffet is a great example. Their habits of saving and living within their means provide a buffer against unexpected expenses or economic downturns.

- **Positive Impact:** Frugality often extends beyond individual benefits to positively impact the community and society as a whole. By reducing consumption and living sustainably, frugal individuals contribute to less resource depletion and a smaller ecological footprint.

- **Generosity:** Surprisingly, frugality can lead to increased generosity. When you have control over your finances and are not burdened by excessive debt or wasteful spending, you have the capacity to help others in need through charitable giving or acts of kindness. Instead of storing up items you don't use anymore at home like your used clothes, books, toys, etc, you can donate it at any donation centre found near you.

- **<u>Personal Growth:</u>** The journey of embracing frugality can lead to personal growth and self-discovery. It encourages self-discipline, goal setting, consistent and continuous learning about financial matters and resource management.

Chapter 1
Budgeting and Planning

Budgeting and planning are essential pillars of sound financial management. They serve as the road-map to achieving your financial goals and aspirations. Whether you're aiming to buy a home, pay off debt, save for your dream vacation, or secure your retirement, a well-thought-out budget and strategic planning are your allies in this journey. If you want to be frugal, then you must have a budget.

A budget is a detailed plan that outlines your income and expenses over a specific period, typically a month. It's a tool that helps you allocate your financial resources efficiently, ensuring that your spending aligns with your priorities; spending below your means. Budgeting allows you to gain a clear picture of where your money goes, how you spend it and empowers you to make informed decisions about your finances.

You can track all your expenses, categorizing them into fixed expenses (e.g., rent/mortgage, utilities) and variable expenses (e.g., groceries, entertainment) by using an expenses tracker logbook and by so doing, you can determine your financial goals and prioritize them. These could include paying off debt, saving for emergencies, or investing for the future. Allocate a portion of your income to each expense category based on your priorities. Make sure to set aside money for savings and investments. Using this strategy is the holy grail to living happily and comfortably at the same time.

There are so many benefits attached to budgeting. This includes:

1. The ability to control your debt and provide structured approach to paying down debt, helping you become debt-free faster.

2. The ability to save and invest ensuring that you're building wealth for the future.

3. This also reduce stress; knowing where your money goes and having a plan in place can reduce your financial stress and anxiety.

While budgeting focuses on day-to-day financial management, having strategic planning takes a longer-term view. It involves setting financial goals and devising a plan to achieve them. Like:

1. Clearly defining your short-term and long-term financial goals, such as buying a nice home; not necessarily big home that would be very expensive to maintain, retiring comfortably, or funding your child's education.

2. Creating a roadmap by breaking down your goals into actionable steps, Determining how much money you need to save or invest and by when.

3. Risk Assessment Or Management: Considering potential risks and challenges that may impact your plan, and develop strategies to mitigate them.

With that been said, periodically review your progress and adjust your plan as needed. Life circumstances and financial markets can change, requiring flexibility in your strategy.

<u>Creating a Frugal Budget</u>
<u>Practical Tips and Examples</u>

Do you know that creating a frugal budget means designing a financial plan that prioritizes savings and conscious spending while minimizing unnecessary expenses. It's about making deliberate choices to live within your means and allocate your resources efficiently. All these have been mentioned earlier but this would be accompanied with practical tips and examples.

The very first on is

1. <u>Access your Income:</u> first and foremost, start by calculating your total monthly income using your expenses logbook. This includes your salary, your side hustle payment(s), your rental income, or other sources of money.

For example: suppose Mr. Franklin just received in monthly salary of $3,000, his side hustle he received $500, then his total monthly income is $3,500.

2. <u>Track your Expenses:</u> Record all your expenses in order for you to know where your money goes. Then categorize your expenses into essential and non-essentials categories.

For example, using Mr. Franklin again, categorizing his expenses as per their worth:

- Rent/Mortgage: $1,200
- Utilities: $150
- Transportation: $200
- Dining out: $100
- Entertainment: $50

● Total Monthly Expenses: $2000

Now imagine if he cooks at home, dining out expenses cost will be very little or no cost at all, that $100 would have been added to his saving box or piggy bank.

3. Set Savings Goals: Determine your financial goal, such as saving for the raining day, or an emergency fund, paying off debt, or saving for that special vacation; probably to Hawaii, Miami, or visiting your family. A portion of your monthly income can be allocated to it.

For Example:
Emergency Fund Savings: $300
Debt Repayment: $200
Vacation Fund: $100
Total Monthly Savings: $600

4. Cut Unnecessary Expenses: Identify areas where you can reduce or eliminate spending. This might include eating out less frequently which I had mentioned earlier, canceling unused subscriptions, or finding cheaper alternatives.You might want to ask ; does it mean I should so deprive myself of these things ? absolutely not! But let there be limit to it. Treat those thing as old monies treat it(I mean the rich like Warren Buffet). In the next chapter, I will explain in details what cutting unnecessary expenses.

For Example:

Reducing Dining Out: $100 → $50
Canceling Unused Streaming Service: $15
Total Monthly Savings from Cutting Expenses:
$65

5. <u>Create a Frugal Grocery List:</u> Plan your meals, buy generic brands, use coupons, and purchase items in bulk to reduce grocery expenses.
For Example:

Previous Grocery Spending: $300 → $250

6. **Use Public Transportation or Carpool:** If possible, use public transit or carpool to reduce fuel and maintenance expenses.

For Example:

Previous Transportation Costs: $200 → $150

7. **Shop Second-hand or Thrift:** Consider purchasing clothing, furniture, and other items from thrift stores or online marketplaces or buying a second-hand car to save on costs

For Example:

Buying Second-hand Furniture: $300 → $150

8. **Review and Adjust:** Regularly review your budget and make adjustments as

needed to ensure you're staying on track in achieving your frugal goals.

For Example:

Monthly Budget Adjustment: Increased savings by $50

Dr. Kristen Amanda

Chapter 2
Cutting Everyday expenses

In this chapter, I will be reviewing the focuses on practical strategies and tips for reducing your everyday expenses, helping you save money in various aspects of your daily life. By implementing the suggestions in this chapter, you can make significant strides towards a more frugal lifestyle. Below are the key points covered in this chapter:

1. **Reducing Utilities Costs:** This section provides guidance on how to lower your utility bills, including electricity, water, and gas. By engaging in utilizing energy-efficient practices, such as using LED light bulbs, sealing drafts, and adjusting thermostat settings,you decrease your monthly utility expenses.

2. **<u>Saving on Transportation:</u>** In this part,I will be explaining to you on how to cut transportation costs, you can own a car and still reduce it maintenance cost. For example, instead of driving to the park or to the grocery store, just take a walk or even ride bicycle; it could be the manual bicycle or the electric bicycle.

3. **<u>Smart Grocery Shopping:</u>** This is one of the quickest ways to prevent food waste while also saving your money. This means fine-tuning your grocery shopping habits so everything you buy gets put to good use to reduce waste. For example creating a shopping lists, using coupons, taking advantage of sales, and purchasing generic or store-brand products to reduce your grocery bills.

4. **<u>Cooking at Home:</u>** Cooking at home is a key component of a frugal lifestyle. Cooking you're your home-made meals can be more

5. cost-effective than dining out, helping you save money and eat healthier.

Chapter 3
Frugal Lifestyle Choices

This chapter brings us to the choices of lifestyle of a frugal person. A frugal person is not wasteful, always saving money on groceries and home goods, makes a budget, rein in entertainment and dining out, finding ways to cost-cut on necessities and loves spending more effectively on self-care; in the aspect of his/her health and wellness and the welfare of his/her family, and a many more to mention but a few.

Minimalism and Decluttering

Embracing minimalism involves decluttering your life; reducing unnecessary things in your home thereby creating enough space for ventilation , and focusing on what truly adds value to your life. By decluttering your living space, you not only create a more organized environment but also avoid needless spending on items that has no meaning to you and won't enhance your life.

DIY Projects and Repairs

DIY(Do-It-Yourself) project and repairs practically involve you fixing partially damaged items like your electric iron, weeding your compound, washing your car, fixing stiffed windows and doors. This is something that can actually be done by yourself. You can acquire this skill yourself and even turn your DIY project to crafting, rather than buying a new one and replacing the old ones. DIY project empower you to create and repair things on your own terms.

Second-Hand Shopping

Thrift stores, garage sales, and online marketplaces offer numerous opportunities to find quality items at significantly lower prices than buying new. You can decide to buy an item during their discount sales like black Friday discount, and the likes. This might seem to distant as you might need that item at that particular time; that brings us to the next point.

Borrowing and Sharing

This popular statements goes like this "there is love in sharing". One of a frugal lifestyle is you will learn the value of borrowing or sharing items with neighbors, friends, and family. Whether it's tools, books, or any household appliances. This practice reduce the need of purchasing items you infrequently use. And if need be, you can still keep on borrowing from your friends, neighbors,and family pending the time any discount opportunity shows up.

This is something I've tried and I am still trying and this is actively helpful.

By adopting this frugal lifestyle, the principle of minimalism, embracing DIY option, trying out the second-hand options, and participating in sharing opportunities, you can significantly reduce your consumption, and cut expenses by half, and lead a more mindful and sustainable life.

Saving For Housing

Do you know that if you live in a middle class street, it will drastically cost-cut your housing costs, one of the most significant expenses in most people's lives. By making informed and rational thought about living in a middle-class street or community, you can accumulate substantial financial savings.

Chapter 4
Renting Vs. Buying

I will briefly discuss with you the pros and cons of renting a home versus buying a home. Me telling you this is to help you understand the financial implications of each option. There are a lot of pros and cons for buying or renting a home. With the list below, this will help you decide whether to consider buying a home or rent a home.

Pros of Renting

1. **Flexibility:** Renting offers flexibility to move when your lease ends, which can be beneficial for those who anticipate frequent relocations for work or personal reasons.

2. **Lower Initial Costs:** Renting typically requires a smaller upfront financial commitment than buying, as you don't need a huge down payment or to cover closing costs.

3. **Fewer Maintenance Responsibilities**: Renters are usually not responsible for major maintenance or repair costs. If something breaks, it's often the landlord's responsibility to fix it.

4. **Predictable Expenses**: Renters can budget more easily, as their monthly rent remains relatively stable, with fewer unexpected expenses related to property maintenance.

<u>Cons of Renting</u>

1. **No Equity Buildup:** Rent payments do not contribute to building equity or ownership in the property. You're essentially

paying for a place to live without the potential for a return on investment.

2. **Limited Control:** Renters have limited control over the property, including restrictions on making significant changes or improvements to the space.

3. **Rent Increases:** Landlords can increase rent prices at the end of the lease, potentially causing financial stress for renters.

4. **Lack of Tax Benefits:** Renters do not enjoy tax benefits like mortgage interest deductions that homeowners can claim.

Pros of Buying

1. **Equity and ownership**: Homeowners build equity over time, which can be a

forced investment. As you pay off your mortgage, you will own more of your home.

2. **Status and control:** You have control over your assets, allowing you to make changes and improvements as you wish.

3. **Potential Appreciation:** Homes can often appreciate in value over time, which can generate income when you sell.

Tax benefits: Homeowners benefit from tax deductions for mortgage interest, property taxes, and certain home-related expenses.

Cons of Buying

1. **Higher initial costs:** Buying a home often requires a larger down payment and can include additional costs such as closing costs, property taxes and homeowners insurance

2. **Maintenance costs:** Homeowners are responsible for all maintenance and repair costs, which can sometimes be unexpected and costly.

3. **Not much flexibility:** Owning a home ties you to a fixed location, making it difficult to relocate for work opportunities or personal reasons.

4. **Market Risk:** The real estate market can be unpredictable, and house prices can plummet, potentially costing you your investment if you need to sell during a recession.

The decision is all yours. Listen to me, owning a private home is more favorable to me as it does not make me an impulse buyer. So you can decide to own a home as long as you have 10% to 15% the value of the house for maintenance or rent a home if you are willing to abide by the rules and regulation of the landlord.

Downsizing

As I said earlier concerning owning a home, downsizing involves moving to a smaller, or cozy, affordable home. This will definitely help as you will gain benefits, such as lower mortgage, reduced maintenance, and simplified living. Nobody knows my net worth in where I live and that is because I am living a simplified and minimalistic life.

Roommates and House Hacking

While I was earning over $500k a year, I still lived with my roommate. I didn't spend my money on buying Lamborghinis, or expensive watches, expensive clothes, etc and that is because I wanted to start a real estate investment. This reduced my housing cost as we both splitted the housing cost. That is because we leveraged house hacking strategy.

Chapter 5
Frugal Entertainment

In this chapter,you will get to know the art of enjoying life without breaking the bank. Preventive entertainment is all about fun, comfort and satisfaction in experiences that don't break your wallet.Some have been listed in the table of content.

There are means whereby you enjoy yourself without breaking your bank and your wallet gives rest to your mind as you would not worry on how you will pay back debt. Some of the means includes:

Free and Low-Cost Activities

There are lots of free and low-cost activities, this includes attending a barbecue party at your neighbor's house, or hosting the barbecue party your self, hiking with your family and friends, visiting local museums, attending cultural events, or even visiting libraries around you. There is happiness being frugal because you don't get to spend more than normal and you will still remain debt free.

Watching Movies on Netflix

Watching movies in a cinema just to show off to others that you are always the first to watch a movie and buying their expensive snacks is likely to break your bank. You might successfully fulfil your desire oppressing them but you won't be happy at the end because the deed has been done already. You can subscribed to streaming subscription like Netflix enjoying a wide variety of content.

Library Resources

Libraries are treasure troves of entertainment options.Reading books, listening to audiobooks, DVDs, and other digital resources are for personal growth.

Library resources enriched lives without spending significant amount of money. Free borrowing of books can contribute to more financial ideas in which you can implement to making your lives better.

Group Discounts

These typically are special pricing arrangement a sales company offered to individuals who purchase their products in bulk. Remember I once said being frugal does not mean you should live a poor lifestyle. Buying a ticket in bulk for your family for entertainment purposes like tickets to a music concert, sporting events, and attraction tours reduces purchase rates and that is because they are bought in large quantities.

Chapter 6
Managing Debt and Interest
Understanding Debt

As a minimalist or a frugal individual as I am, you must know how to handle any debt. Don't get me wrong there are two types of debt: the good debt and the bad debt.

The good debt is the type of debt used as a leverage to start any investment. Note this; you borrowing money in the bank to add to your capital you want to use to start up an investment is a wise startup because in the end, you are likely to recover the money borrowed from the bank and you will still be earning more profit from your particular business. While

The bad debt is the type of debt used for consumption. Loaning a debt for consumption is very dangerous and that is because you are likely to go deeper into more debt. To repay your debt becomes a problem for you. I strongly advice you not to go into debt for the purpose of consumption. Whenever possible, make extra payments towards your debts. Even small additional payments can significantly reduce the total interest you pay over time.

Be cautious about taking on new debt while you're working to pay off existing debt. Responsible credit use involves using credit wisely and not accumulating new debt.

Instead of accumulating debt, build an emergency fund to avoid unexpected expenses. Also, regularly review your debt repayment plan and adjust it as needed as soon as possible. Better still, consider consulting a financial counselor or debt management agency if you are overwhelmed by debt with huge interest.

Paying Off High-Interest Rates

One of the primary goals of managing debt is to pay off high-interest debt as quickly as possible. The chapter provides strategies for prioritizing and tackling debt with the highest interest rates first.

Payment of debt should definitely start from the one with the highest interest rate first, then the medium interest rate to the lowest interest.

Negotiating Lower Interest Rates

Negotiating with creditors is another way of managing interest rate. Before negotiating, gather all the necessary information about your debt, including the current interest rate, outstanding balance, and payment history. Know your credit score, as it can impact your negotiating power. After a thorough research about your debt, craft a clear and concise request for the interest rate reduction, be polite and professional when speaking with any customer service representatives on phone call or the creditor's website.

Explain your situation and the reason for requesting an interest rate reduction. Common reasons include financial hardship even when you know you still have more as a backup, a good payment history as you are the type of person that is comfortable, or the availability of better offers from other creditors.

Lay emphasis on your commitment to repaying the debt and the benefit to the creditor in granting your request. For example, the creditor would earn 3% to 5% of your profit in the business you want to venture into and in return you pay no task.

Chapter 7
Frugal transportation

In this Chapter I will be discussing how to be frugal even in transportation, yes, you heard me. I know some of you might have seen in your community where in a family the parent can decide to go on public transport rather than going with their cars and that got you thinking "Is their vehicle faulty? Are they broke again?" That is not true n this case. This means they are making thoughtful, money-saving choices when it comes to how they travel, whether for their daily commute, errands, or leisure activities.

Of course that is who I am. I rarely go out with my car because I spend time in my mini office observing this and writing things down until it becomes a book like this one.

One of the ways being frugal in transport are as follows:

Utilizing Public Transit

Considering public transportation like buses, subways, trams, or commuter trains which is way better instead of driving your car, getting stuck in traffic, and paying for gas, maintenance and parking fee, You are opting for a more budget-friendly mode of travel. Give a thought to that.

Carpooling With Others

Another thing to discuss here is about carpooling with others. Let's say you and your neighbor or someone who live nearby your community have similar destination with you, possibly can share a single vehicle with them as it cut down expenses on fuel and maintenance. By adopting frugal transportation practices like carpooling, you not only save money but also foster a sense of communal trust among yourself, your neighbors, and even those from neighboring communities who share a single vehicle.

Choosing Biking or Walking

I left my home for a nearby grocery store, and I decided to ride my bike there,on when I left my garage to the grocery store, my neighbor said to me "hey, are you taking a stroll ? " I told him "Of course not, I am on my way to the grocery store." then he said "that's where I am actually heading to. Hop in let us go together." then I said to him " No thank you. This is a sunny day and I would love to go to the grocery store on my bike. I just got it yesterday. Besides, I need to release some of my metabolic waste through sweat. Also, I want to be part of those that will encourage eco-friendly environment." Shocked by what I said, he said to me " Okay you are right tho. I notice I am getting fat below my belly button. Hold on please, let me also get my bike."

You see   I just influence my neighbor's life and improved his knowledge about encouraging a carbon-free environment. He did not use go with his car to the grocery store.   Do not get me wrong, I do not mean you should abandon your car you can still drive it especially when you are travelling with your family or you want to buy in bulk. Better still get an electric or hybrid car which means fewer or not trip to the gas station and less money is spent on fuel.

Chapter 8
Saving on health and wellness

Do you know you can effectively manage their health and wellness expenses while adhering to a frugal lifestyle. I priotize my health more than any other thing so you should do so too.

Preventive Health Measures

Eating a balanced diet is a significant step towards good health and you can achieve this without breaking the bank. Just focus on affordable nutrient-rich foods. Example of an affordable balanced diet includes:

- **Incorporate Whole Foods:** Base your meals around affordable whole foods like rice, beans, oats, lentils, and seasonal fruits and vegetables. These items are often cost-effective and provide essential nutrients. This is still better than taking in junks.

- **Buy in Bulk:** Purchase staples goods like grains, legumes, and frozen vegetables in bulk to reduce per-serving costs.
- **Plan Meals:** Create meal planner using an effective ingredients efficiently and by so doing reducing food waste. This is one of the best option you would not find in any book on frugality living.
- **Cook at Home:** Preparing meals at home is typically cheaper than dining out. It also gives you control over ingredients and portion sizes.

Always staying hydrated is vital for good health as it help in digesting food quickly and in releasing of metabolic waste. You would want to carry along with you a reusable water bottle and fill it with tap water. It is not only cost-effective but also very eco-friendly.

Regular physical activities like your house chores, gardening, etc is also essential for preventing various health issues rather than given out the work to maids. Also, you do not need an expensive gym membership to stay active.

There are Outdoor activities like walking, jogging, hiking, or playing sport at local parks. And engaging in home workouts; do you know there are many free or low-cost workout routine online. Believe me you I do not have a single gym membership I make use of one of the online workout routine. I bought myself dumbbells and also make good use of my household items.

Mental Health and Stress Management

Apart from eating an affordable balanced diet, you need to also check your mental health. According to the World Health Organization (WHO), approximately 1 in 4 people will experience a mental health issue at some point in their lives. This statistic highlights the widespread impact of mental health challenges on individuals and communities around the world. Mental health issues affect people of all ages, backgrounds, and walks of life, making them a significant public health concern. It underscores the importance of raising awareness, providing support, and promoting access to mental health services to address this global health challenge effectively. So do not ignore this.

Anyways, there are some strategies in which you can maintain balance between living your frugal lifestyle and your mental well-being.

- **Prioritize Self-Care:** Allocate time for self-care activities that promote mental health, such as exercises, meditation, mindfulness, and relaxation techniques. Many of these practices are cost-free or require minimal investment so you do not have to worry whether you are still living a frugal lifestyle or not.

- **Build a Support System:** Lean on your social network for emotional support. Engage in meaningful relationships with friends and family, which can provide a strong foundation for emotional well-being without requiring extravagant spending.

- **Set Realistic Financial Goals:** Establish clear financial goals and budgets that align with your frugal lifestyle.

Knowing where your money is going and having financial stability can reduce anxiety and stress.

<u>Generic Medications</u>

Another keyword on saving on health and wellness is generic medication. Generic medication is a type of pharmaceutical drug that is equivalent to a brand-name medication in terms of active ingredients, dosage, safety, quality, and intended use. This means you choose more cost-efficient generic drugs over expensive brand-name medications, thus you save money without compromising on health. And if you decide to go with high brand-name drugs, then that is good for you. You can conduct your pharmacist who could prescribed alternative drug for you.

Remember, using generic medication does not mean you are using a less quality medication, It is very well just as safe and effective as the original, but at a lower cost.

You can further reduce your out-of-pocket expenses when you make use of generic medications which offers lower co-pays.

Health Insurance Tips

Health insurance is very crucial at any stage, especially as you get older. Attending to this earlier will prevent you breaking your piggy bank set up for your kids college fee. It provides financial protection against unexpected medical expenses. I will list some of the key health insurance tips I use while still maintaining my frugal lifestyle which I strongly believe it would be one of your key reason did not regret buying this book:

1. **Assess Your Needs:** Start up by evaluating your healthcare needs. Find out about your current health status, any ongoing medical conditions, and the likelihood of needing specialized care. This

assessment will help you choose a plan that aligns with your specific requirements without breaking your piggy bank.

2. **Compare Plans:** go round and compare health insurance plans between other health insurance plans. Look at both premiums (the amount you pay for coverage) and out-of-pocket costs (deductibles, co-pays, and co-insurance). A plan with a lower premium may have higher out-of-pocket costs, so weigh the overall cost carefully.

3. **Understand the Network:** Paying attention to the network of healthcare providers associated with the plan is another step you really need to follow. Staying in-network often results in lower costs. Check if your current healthcare providers are in-network, especially if you have doctors you prefer to see.

4. Consider High Deductible Plans: High-deductible health plans (HDHPs) can be cost-effective for individuals who are generally healthy. It is a preventive measure to the generally healthy. They typically have lower premiums but higher deductibles. Pairing an HDHP with a Health Savings Account (HSA) can offer tax advantages and help you save for future healthcare expenses.

5. Check for Preventive Care Coverage: Many health insurance plans cover preventive services at no additional cost. This can include vaccinations, screenings, and annual check-ups. Take advantage of these benefits to maintain your health and catch potential issues early.

6. Explore Telehealth Options: Telehealth services are increasingly popular, and can be a cost-effective way to get treatment, especially for minor issues or routine checkups Confirm that your insurance plan covers telehealth visits.

7. **Review Prescription Drug Coverage**: If you take regular medications, review the plan's prescription drug coverage. Look for plans that offer affordable co-pays or discounts on prescription drugs you commonly use. Consider generic alternatives when possible. I had already mentioned that earlier.

8. **Consider Catastrophic Coverage as a choice:** Depending on your health and financial situation, catastrophic health insurance might be an option. These plans have low premiums but high deductibles and are primarily designed to protect you against any major medical expenses.

9. **Stay Informed:** Keep yourself informed always about any changes to your insurance plan. Review your plan documents, including the Summary of your Benefits and Coverage, and stay updated on any policy

changes, especially during the open enrollment period.

10. **Maximize Preventive Care:** Focus on the preventive health measures to reduce the likelihood of you needing costly medical treatments. Maintain a healthy lifestyle through regular exercise, a balanced diet, and stress management to lower your overall healthcare expenses.

Emergency Fund: Always have an emergency fund to cover unexpected medical expenses or costs associated with your high-deductible plans. Having savings set aside can prevent financial strain during any of your medical emergencies.

Always Ask Questions: Do not hesitate to ask your insurance provider questions about your coverage, claims, or billing.

Understanding your policy thoroughly can help you make informed decisions and avoid unexpected costs.

Chapter 9
Frugal Travel

One of my favourite, I love going on vacations with my family and I never have any rethink on every decision I made. I will give you the methods I used in for that:

1. **Plan and Budget:** First and foremost, I planned my realistic travel budget for myself and my family; the amount of money I can comfortably afford to spend during my vacation without jeopardizing my financial goals.

2. **Choose Affordable Destinations:** Opt for destinations where your money will go

further. Consider countries with a lower cost of living, budget-friendly accommodations, and affordable transportation.

3. Use Travel Apps and Guides: making good use of travelling app to find deals on accommodations, transportations, and other activities that you would love. Apps like Skyscanner, Airbnb, and TripAdvisor can help you plan and by so doing saving of the cost of meeting disappointment. The same also goes to the use of travel guide.

Chapter 10
Investing and Growing wealth

In this Chapter, I will be explaining in details on the principles of frugal investing and wealth-building strategies. We all have heard about investing and wealth growing or probably have heard the word "Invest" .

The term "investing" refers to the act of allocating money or resources to an asset with the expectation of generating income or profit in the future. You can invest your money on various financial instrument such as stocks: Apple, Tesla, S&P500, NASDAC,etc ; bonds, real estate, mutual funds, and retirement account, instead of lavishing your current funds on liablity that will become of no value in latter end.

Growing wealth on the other hand, is the process of increasing your financial assets and net worth over time through investments and other strategic financial decisions.

This two definition giving with examples alone can boost your morale on increasing your wealth and at the same time still be enjoying your financial lifestyle as it builds a financial cushion and stability to handle unexpected expenses.

Smart Investment Choices

There are so many investment options around the globe such as stocks, bonds, mutual funds, real estate. Successful investing involves making choices that meet your unique needs today and your financial goal in the future. It starts with knowing yourself; if you want to invest in short-term investment, like saving for vacation or a car, or long-term like retirement. Remember that it is all about risk and I am not in the best place to give that type of advice. I am not a financial adviser and I will recommend that your consult your financial adviser before making any financial decisions.

Retirement Planning

This involves the determining retirement income goals and what is needed to achieve those goals. Retirement planning includes identifying income sources, sizing up expenses, implementing a saving program, and managing assets and risk.

As a frugal individual working in a 9 to 5 job, which can be stressful most times and tiring, this is for you. You can start up a saving program or open a retirement accounts and 401(k)s, while still living below your means. Within 6 to 10 years, you will be sitting comfortably in your fine condo living the life you have been dreamed about.

<u>Frugal Investment Apps</u>

There are multiple apps online you can purchase stocks and manage your money in the financial markets, which includes stocks, bonds, cryptocurrencies, and mutual funds. Investment apps like Binance, FXTM, Charles Schwab, etc offer you an easy and convenient way to purchase, manage your investment, track your portfolio performance and make informed investment decisions.

Chapter 11
Frugal Parenting

You might be wondering how frugality involves the parent. Yes, it does involve parenting. Frugal parenting involves raising children in a financially responsible manner, making mindful choices to provide for their needs while staying within a budget.

In this chapter, I will delve into practical strategies and tips for parents who wants to raise happy, healthy children without breaking the bank.

Budget-Friendly Kids Activities

We all know kids will want to celebrate something, weather it's their birthday party or tea party or a homecoming party. There are several budget-friendly options to choose from! Consider hosting a DIY craft party as a birthday party for your kids, or a backyard camping adventure in a playground with picnic table, or a movie marathon. These ideas not only keep costs down without expensive toys or gadges but also provide unique and memorable experiences for your kids and the well wishers.

Hand-Me-Downs And Thrift Shopping

The reusing of toys, clothes and baby gear from older siblings or other families are one of the great ways to reducing waste. Second-hand shopping keep the environment out of landfills and extending their lifespan.

This strategy, if implemented by the parent to their children, will prevent them growing up thinking that it's okay to toss out anything we do not need any longer. As noted above, it is not good for the environment, but it also makes it difficult to teach your kids the value of the stuff in your lives. When we receive and share hand-me-downs, it helps teach our kids that our possessions are valuable. Even though the items are used, another child (or adult) is able to benefit from them.

Financial Education For Kids

Many parents find It uncomfortable discussing money when their kids are around them. When their kids become adults and leave home, they face heavy financial responsibilities, including creating a budget and choosing the right investments for their long-term goals. Much of the time, however, they are woefully unprepared for those challenges.

You should start teaching your kids how to be financially independent at a very tender age for them not to be ignorant of how finances work.

NOTE: I AM NOT A FINANCIAL ADVISER. MAKE SURE TO CONSULT YOUR FINANCIAL ADVISER FOR FINANCIAL ADVICE

<u>Conclusion</u>

<u>Embracing a Frugal Lifestyle</u>

Sacrifice, by definition, is not fun. The key to embracing a frugality rather than tolerating it is in identifying your motivation for practicing it. What life values is your frugality helping you fulfill? What are you able to do with the money that you free up through practicing frugality? That should be the question that you should ask yourself before practicing it.

Personally, I wanted to handle my money responsible. Being responsible is very important to me, and when I started grad school that translated into living within my means, being financially independent from my parents, and starting to save for retirement which I have been practicing since childhood. I learned to practice frugality in each of my budget categories, and it was satisfying because I believed that in doing so I was becoming more responsible. Money that I no longer spend on my everyday living expenses could be put into savings.

I implore every reader of this book to follow the strategy to the letter.

<u>Achieving Financial Freedom</u>

I became financially secured when I reached 25, and financially free at 30. Though, many people in their 20s are already financially free, but it's possible. Working toward financial security need not be an exercise in self-deprivation, though many people assume it to be.

<u>Appendix</u>
<u>Recommended Books Related To</u>
<u>Frugal Living</u>

1. **The Total Money Makeover** by Dave Ramsey:
A practical and motivating guide to financial fitness, offering step-by-step advice on getting out of debt, building emergency funds, and investing wisely.

2. **Your Money or Your Life** by Vicki Robin and Joe Dominguez:

A seminal work on transforming your relationship with money and achieving financial independence. This book emphasizes aligning your spending with your values and pursuing a purposeful life.

3.**The Millionaire Next Door** by Thomas J. Stanley and William D. Danko:
Based on extensive research, this book explores the habits of wealthy individuals and provides insights into living below your means, investing wisely, and accumulating wealth.

4. **Essentialism: The Disciplined Pursuit of Less** by Greg McKeown:
While not solely about frugality, this book explores the concept of

essentialism, encouraging readers to focus on what truly matters and eliminate non-essentials, aligning perfectly with a frugal lifestyle.

5.**Simplicity Parenting** by Kim John Payne and Lisa M. Ross:
For parents interested in frugal parenting, this book offers practical advice on simplifying family life, reducing clutter, and fostering meaningful connections with children.

6. **Blogs and Websites**:
Explore online resources such as Mr. Money Mustache, The Simple Dollar, and Frugalwoods. These platforms offer a wealth of articles, personal stories, and frugal living tips shared by experienced practitioners.

7. **Documentary:**

Watch the documentary "Minimalism: A Documentary About the Important Things" on platforms like Netflix. It explores the lives of minimalists and their pursuit of a meaningful life with less stuff.

Dr. Kristen Amanda

www.ingramcontent.com/pod-product-compliance
Lightning Source LLC
Chambersburg PA
CBHW071059290526
45795CB00004B/1574